David BECKHAM

By Jeff Bradley

The
Child's World
www.childsworld.com

Published in the United States of America by The Child's World®
1980 Lookout Drive • Mankato, MN 56003-1705
800-599-READ • www.childsworld.com

ACKNOWLEDGMENTS

The Child's World®: Mary Berendes, Publishing Director

Produced by Shoreline Publishing Group LLC
President / Editorial Director: James Buckley, Jr.
Designer: Tom Carling, carlingdesign.com
Assistant Editor: Jim Gigliotti

Photo Credits: Cover: Corbis.
Interior: AP/Wide World: 3, 5, 8, 15, 19, 24, 27; Getty Images: 1, 7, 11, 12, 16, 20, 23, 28.

LIBRARY OF CONGRESS
CATALOGING-IN-PUBLICATION DATA

Bradley, Jeff.
  David Beckham / by Jeff Bradley.
     p. cm. — (The world's greatest athletes)
  Includes index.
  ISBN 978-1-59296-879-4 (library bound : alk. paper)
  1. Beckham, David, 1975- 2. Soccer players—England—Biography.
  3. Celebrities—England—Biography. I. Title. II. Series.

  GV942.7.B432B73 2008
  796.334092—dc22
  [B]

                                        2007032022

CONTENTS

Lights, Camera, Action!

THE HOTEL BALLROOM IN LOS ANGELES WAS packed with reporters from dozens of countries. Photographers and television cameramen stood shoulder to shoulder to record the event. The reporters were from the worlds of sports, TV, movies, and music. Only one thing was missing: the celebrity. That was soccer player David Beckham, who was not even in Los Angeles! He wasn't even in the United States!

David was in Madrid, Spain. He played for a team called Real (RAY-uhl) Madrid, one of the best soccer **clubs** in the world. David appeared at the event that day on a huge television screen.

Still, no one seemed to care that David was not there in person. The big news was that he was leaving Spain to play . . . in the United States!

Why was this big news? Because David, one of the most popular soccer players ever, had signed to play for the Los Angeles Galaxy of Major League Soccer (MLS) for $250 million for five seasons!

How could that be? How could a soccer player make so much money in the United States, where sports such as football, baseball, basketball, and NASCAR are way more popular? The Galaxy play in MLS, which is not nearly as popular as those other sports. The answer is that David is more than just a soccer player. For nearly 15 years, this 31-year-old Englishman has dazzled fans with his amazing, right-footed kicks. But his good looks, always-changing hairstyles, and famous pop star wife have made David more than just an athlete. A favorite of fans of all ages all over the globe, he has become a world superstar. Now he has a new mission: to make soccer huge in the United States.

Welcome to America! David joined the Los Angeles Galaxy in 2007.

CHAPTER 1

Kicking in the Park

LONG BEFORE DAVID BECKHAM CAME TO AMERICA, he was a skinny boy who loved football—that's what they call soccer in England. David played the game day and night in his East London neighborhood. "I'm going to play for Manchester United," he first told his parents when he was just three years old.

Manchester United, much like Real Madrid, is a world-famous soccer team. The club plays before sellout crowds in Manchester, England, but is loved by fans all over the world. David, who was born on May 2, 1975, in Leytonstone, England, was a fan of United from an early age because his father, Ted, once gave him a United uniform for Christmas.

David was always kicking a ball around. "I was murdering the flowerbeds in the backyard," he says.

David fulfilled a childhood dream when he played nine seasons for the famous Manchester United team.

He also played at Chase Lane Park, just around the corner from his house. David's dad also played there for a team called Kingfisher. David loved to tag along to his father's games. "After he got back from his job as a heating **engineer**, we'd go to the park and

Practice makes perfect: Thanks to a lot of hard work, David can control the ball just about any way he wants.

just practice for hours on end," David wrote in his **autobiography**, *David Beckham, Both Feet on the Ground.* "We'd work on touch [control of the ball] and kicking the ball properly until it was too dark to see."

All the practice paid off. David became a star player for a youth team called Ridgeway Rovers. At first, he was a little scared of his big, tough coach. "If you weren't playing well, he would tell you were **rubbish** and needed to do better," David wrote. "But he wasn't one of those dads who stood on the **touchline** [sideline] screaming. He had a softness about him as well."

The Rovers worked hard and became a great team. The boys were not even teenagers yet, but it was clear that several of them would become **professional** players, especially David. Even though he was as skinny as a toothpick, he was one of the best young players in East London. It's normal in England for young players to practice with pro teams very early. However, David's father said that his son would not do so until he was in high school.

When David began attending Chingford School, he faced a serious problem. Chingford did not have a soccer team! "They played rugby instead of

English teams can offer youngsters "schoolboy" contracts. That means they can practice with the pro teams, but don't get paid.

Young David Beckham

> David's Rovers team traveled to play games in Germany and the Netherlands!

> David was a cross-country and swimming champ for Chingford High School.

> His favorite subject in school was art, and David loved to sketch Disney characters as a kid.

> David sang solos in the school choir.

> When David was 13, his school team traveled to the United States and played against American teams in Texas. It was his first trip to the United States.

soccer," David remembered. Rugby is a popular sport in England. It looks a lot like American NFL-style football, only with no protective pads. David and his friends convinced the rugby coach to help them form a soccer team. Soon, Chingford was winning league championships.

"Maybe the soccer helped me be happy there," David wrote. "I wasn't that interested in lessons. There was only one thing I ever wanted to do with my life." David wanted to be a soccer player.

When he was 14, David's dreams started to come true. There are many pro teams in London, and they all wanted to sign David. But there was only one team David wanted to play for, ever since that Christmas when he saw that bright red shirt under the tree. That team was Manchester United. On July 8, 1991, David Robert Joseph Beckham signed with the team of his dreams.

David spends a lot of time in the U.S. and in Britain teaching kids who dream about playing soccer just as he once dreamed.

David was only 20 years old when he first broke into Manchester United's starting lineup in 1995.

CHAPTER 2

Living the Dream

FROM THE MOMENT BECKHAM JOINED "MAN U,"
as the team is sometimes called, he saw his life
change in a big way. The life of a "footballer," or pro
soccer player, is a roller-coaster ride—exciting, but
full of ups and downs. First, David and Man U's youth
team won the Football Assocation (FA) Youth Cup,
the most important tournament for English players
under 17. United beat a London team, Crystal Palace,
3–1 and 3–2 in the two-game series.

In the first game in that series, David scored
a fantastic goal with his left foot. While David has
scored a few more goals with his left foot, it was
his right foot that would become one of the most
dangerous weapons in soccer. There were two
main ways he used his right foot to terrorize his

opponents. The first was with long passes to the front of the goal. His teammates could then aim those "**crosses**" into the net. More goals are scored on crosses than on any other play in the game.

David's crossing skills are incredible. It almost seems like he has radar in his foot. He can kick the ball from 30 to 40 yards (27 to 36 m) away and place it wherever he wants.

The second way David's right foot excels is on **free kicks**. A soccer team gets a free kick when a foul is committed against it. The referee blows his whistle and stops the game. A player on the team that was fouled gets to kick the ball. No one from the other team is allowed within 10 yards of him. When free kicks occur near the other team's goal, it can be a great chance for a player to score. David uses his radar-like right foot to aim for places where the goalkeeper can't stop the ball. David's best shots are made with huge curves. By using the inside part of his right foot and swiveling his hips quickly as he kicked the ball, David is able to make the ball curve very sharply! These kicks are his trademark.

"As soon as a free kick is given and it's anywhere near the box, I get excited," David says. "I don't

On this free kick, Beckham has "bent" the ball into the upper corner of the goal, far out of the goalie's reach.

really concentrate on what side the goalkeeper is on, because I always think that if I kick it as well as I can, then I can beat him whichever way he goes."

In January of 1993, when David was still only 17, Manchester United decided to make him a full professional. David would be paid to do what he loved more than anything: play soccer! Before he would become a player on the top team, however, David would have to pay his dues.

The next step up from his youth team was the reserve team. David played there for most of the 1993-94 season. He did get one chance with the first team, in a game against a team called Galatasaray (from the city of Istanbul, Turkey). Early in the second half, the ball was passed to David, and he saw a chance to shoot. "Even though I didn't really connect properly," David remembered, "the ball bobbled in somehow." David ran toward the packed stands to celebrate! A goal in his first start for Manchester United! It was incredible.

David began to wonder if it was now his time to be a star. Soon after that first goal, he got his answer—but not one he expected. Alex Ferguson, Man U's manager (the British word for coach), made

David knows it's time to celebrate when his kicks find the back of the net!

David a starting player—but not for United! Ferguson wanted David to play for a London team called Preston North End. That team played in the English

In His Own Words

▶ *"When I was a kid, I changed my hairstyle as many times as my mom let me, which wasn't often. I remember the first time she took me to the hairdresser, I wanted it really short but she wouldn't let me—she gave me the spiky thing. When I look back I can't believe she did that to me!"*

▶ *"It doesn't freak me out to be so famous. People turn around to me and say, 'Don't you hate it?' How can you hate it? People want your picture, your autograph. It's an honor to have that, to have the ability to make people happy. It doesn't freak me out . . . unless they come up and start crying."*

▶ *"The American Dream is founded on the same principles as my own: If you work hard enough, there never needs to be a limit on how far life can take you. I was born loving soccer and, thanks to my parents, teammates, teachers, and coaches, I've been able to experience some amazing things in my career."*

Third Division, which is like a baseball player going back to the minors!

"They want to get rid of me," David remembers thinking to himself. As it turned out, David's dreams were not over. They were only beginning.

CHAPTER 3

The Highs and Lows

AS IT TURNED OUT, MANCHESTER UNITED DID NOT want to get rid of David. They wanted him to get more action in games and to help him improve as a player. His move to Preston North End was **temporary**. United was letting Preston borrow David for a while, but he would go back to Manchester as soon as the club felt he was ready.

It did not take long. When the 1995-96 season opened, 20-year old David was the starting right **midfielder** for Manchester United. Like a shooting star, his career took off.

In his first season, David scored five goals and helped United win the English **Premier League** title and the FA Cup. The FA Cup is a tournament open to all teams, professional and **amateur**, in England.

David helped Manchester United reach new heights, winning numerous titles and becoming even more popular worldwide.

That's David (left) and teammate David Neville posing with the trophy for Manchester United's Premier League title in 1996.

Winning both titles in one year is called winning "The Double." Only a handful of teams have pulled off that feat.

A year later, United made it back-to-back Premier League titles. By now, the young, blond boy with the awesome crosses and free kicks was becoming a huge fan favorite. During the first game of the 1996-97 season, David scored the goal that made people really pay attention to him. From just inside the midfield line, some 50 yards (45.72 m) from the goal, David decided to attempt the impossible. "The ball was in the air for what seemed to be ages," Beckham wrote in his autobiography. "Sailing toward the goal before it dropped over [the goalkeeper] and into the net. I couldn't have known it then, but that goal was the start of it all: the attention, the press coverage, the fame. It changed forever that afternoon, with one swing of the boot." (English players called their soccer shoes "boots.")

Indeed, it did. Like fireworks flashing on the Fourth of July, David Beckham's name and face were suddenly everywhere in England. He began to date a pop star named Victoria Adams, who was better known as Posh Spice in a group called The Spice Girls. He began to change his hairstyle once or twice a season, going from long and bleached blond, to shaved nearly bald, to long, but in a ponytail. As much as he was making headlines in newspapers for his amazing plays on the soccer field, he was becoming a celebrity as big as any movie star or rock star in the world. Companies wanted to put his face on commercials. Photographers wanted to take his picture for magazine covers.

His career hit a peak in 1998, when David was asked to play for England in the World Cup, the most important competition in soccer. That event is held every four years between the top 32 national teams. Soccer players are paid to play for their pro clubs, but they play for their national team for love of the sport and their country.

England hadn't won the world title since 1966, but it believed that the 1998 team had a chance to win it all. As it turned out, however, David's roller-coaster ride was still racing along at full speed. David expected to start for England. Just as the tournament was about to begin, though, England manager Glenn Hoddle pulled a surprise. He told David he did not think the young Man U star was fully focused on soccer, so he put him on the bench.

England won its first match in the World Cup but lost its second. In the third game, against Colombia, Hoddle put David into the starting lineup. What did David do? He scored on one of his signature free kicks as England won 2-0 to advance into the second round of the tournament. It was a great moment that was about to be followed by the strangest event in David's career.

The World Cup is so popular that in 2006 an estimated 715 million viewers all over the globe saw Italy beat France in the final match.

The game between England and Argentina in the 1998 World Cup was one for the ages. The two teams battled back and forth, thrilling the crowd with fantastic passing and goals. Just after halftime, with the score tied 2-2, David was knocked to the ground. A player for Argentina named Diego Simeone then

This is the England World Cup team that advanced to the second round in 1998. David is on the bottom row at the left.

annoyed David by ruffling his hair. David reacted by trying to kick Simeone. Television viewers could hardly see what Beckham had done, but the referee saw it and immediately gave Beckham a red card. The red card is soccer's worst penalty. It meant that he was kicked out of the game, and that England would have to play the rest of the game with one less player than Argentina. England went on to lose the game and David, who cried in his father's arms after the match, was blamed for the defeat by many fans in England. A national hero had become a villain.

Of course, the story doesn't end there. David admitted his mistake and got on with his career. Soon, he was helping lead Manchester United to the most amazing season in its 121-year history. In 1999, United did one better than "The Double." The club added victory in the European

David and his wife, Victoria, make news with their fashion statements.

Champions League, a title United had not won in 31 years. (The Champions League is a tournament played by the number-one clubs in all European countries.) David also married Victoria, and they had their first son, Brooklyn, who was born in 1999. The Beckhams have had two more sons, Romeo (2002) and Cruz (2005).

David had put his World Cup sorrow behind him. He worked his way back to being a superstar on and off the field, mixing his amazing free kicks and crosses in with fancy clothes and cars that kept his fans wondering just where his picture would show up next.

In 2002, David not only returned to the World Cup, but he also was named England's captain, which he called the greatest honor of his career. Then, in 2003, David decided to move away from Manchester United, signing a contract to play with Real Madrid. Based in Spain, that team was full of the world's best and richest players. The move to Real Madrid proved that David Beckham was willing to take risks and face new challenges.

That brings the story back to Los Angeles and his decision to join the Galaxy in the summer of 2007.

In November of 2003, Queen Elizabeth II presented David with a special honor: the OBE (Officer of the Order of the British Empire).

David's Big Moment

Countries don't just show up at the World Cup to play. Except for two countries—the one that hosts the event and the one that won the previous World Cup—they have to earn their way into the biggest soccer tournament on earth. To do so, they have a playoff against other national teams from their region of the world. In 2001, England was trying to earn its place in the 2002 World Cup. The team needed to at least tie Greece to secure its trip to Japan and South Korea to compete for the Cup.

Trailing 2-1 with time running out in the match, Beckham, the captain, chose the perfect moment to show the type of leader he was.

David, who was nearly perfect during the game with his passing and playmaking, stood 25 yards from the Greece goal. He knew that a successful free kick would put England in the 2002 World Cup. It was time to "Bend it Like Beckham," as the title of a popular movie said.

"I'd missed a few that afternoon," David recalled. "But I wasn't going to give this last one up. I knew this was our last chance."

With 66,000 fans holding their breath, and millions of people watching on TV at home, David curled a

laser-beam of a shot into the upper corner of the net.
"The moment I made contact," David remembered, "I
knew this one was in."

England was in, too—the 2002 World Cup! It was
David's greatest moment in an England jersey.

Even though Beckham had written that "soccer's time is about to come" in the United States, few believed he would make the move to Major League Soccer so soon. But the league's owners decided that the time was right to bring David's soccer skills and off-field popularity to the United States, even if the cost was huge.

"David Beckham is a global sports icon who will make more people aware of soccer in America," said MLS Commissioner Don Garber. "His decision to continue his career in Major League Soccer proves that America is becoming a true 'Soccer Nation.'"

Said Beckham: "If I didn't believe I could make a difference and take soccer to a different level, I wouldn't be doing this."

On July 21, 2007, David made his debut for the Galaxy in a **friendly** against visiting Chelsea. The mission was under way!

David showcased his all-around skills in his first game with the Galaxy.

David Beckham's Career Statistics

Year	Team	Games	Goals	Year	Team	Games	Goals
1994-95*	Manchester	4	0	2000-01	Manchester	43	9
	Preston NE	5	2		England	5	2
	England	1	1	2001-02	Manchester	41	16
1995-96	Manchester	35	7		England	9	2
1996-97	Manchester	46	9	2002-03	Manchester	44	9
	England	9	0	2003-04	Real Madrid	39	4
1997-98	Manchester	45	9	2004-05	Real Madrid	38	4
	England	9	1	2005-06	Real Madrid	37	2
1998-99	Manchester	46	8		England	3	0
	England	5	0	2006-07 #	Real Madrid	23	3
1999-2000	Manchester	43	8		LA Galaxy	8	1
	England	11	0		England	3	0

* Championship: Manchester United – 4 Games, European Competition: 1 Goal, 1 Game (Champions League). # Through 2007 Galaxy season.

GLOSSARY

amateur   somebody who does something for pleasure rather than for pay

autobiography   the story of someone's life written or narrated by that same person

clubs   more than just the "teams," they are the organizations that run soccer teams

crosses   soccer passes that come from the sides across or into the goal area

engineer   somebody who operates or services machines

free kicks   a kick awarded to one team after a foul is called on the other team by the referee

friendly   a soccer a match that does not count in any official standings

midfielder   a soccer player who is active at both ends of the field

Premier League   the top pro soccer league in England

professional   a person who is paid to play a sport

rubbish   trash, junk, or in this case, a poor player

temporary   lasting for just a short time

touchline   the sideline of a soccer field

BOOKS

David Beckham's Soccer Skills
By David Beckham
New York: Collins, 2007.
In this book, the star himself tells young readers about his experiences playing soccer and shares his knowledge about the game.

The Everything Kids' Soccer Book
By Deborah W. Crisfield
Holbrook, Massachusetts: Adams Media Corporation, 2002.
Learn more about the skills and strategies of soccer, including drills and tips for learning to play the game.

Eyewitness Books: Soccer
By DK Publishing
New York: DK Children, 2005.
Learn about the history of soccer and the tools of the sport, including souvenirs and soccer gear from around the world.

WEB SITES

Visit our Web page for lots of links about David Beckham and soccer: www.childsworld.com/links

Note to Parents, Teachers, and Librarians: We routinely check our Web links to make sure they're safe, active sites—so encourage your readers to check them out!

INDEX

ABOUT THE AUTHOR

Jeff Bradley is a senior writer with ESPN *The Magazine*. He has covered soccer for many years, including four World Cups. He has also written about baseball, hockey, golf, and many other sports. He lives (and coaches youth soccer and baseball) in Manasquan, New Jersey, with his wife, Linda, and sons Tyler and Beau.